knit
PINK

25 Patterns to Knit for Comfort, Gratitude, and Charity

LORNA MISER

Martingale®
Create with Confidence

Dedication

In honor of my dear friend Michele Wyman. Breast cancer took her from us, but her talent and memory live on. Michele was a prolific knitwear designer and a friend who helped me grow. Ironically, Michele was not fond of the color pink and she didn't want to live in the shadow of the cause it represents. She was concerned that she would be seen as part of a big pink stereotype and lose her personal identity. She didn't want to be identified as "Michele with breast cancer," but rather as Michele the mom, designer, businesswoman, and teacher. I learned much from Michele and was blessed to have her in my life.

Knit Pink: 25 Patterns to Knit
for Comfort, Gratitude, and Charity
© 2013 by Lorna Miser

Create with Confidence

Martingale®
19021 120th Ave. NE, Ste. 102
Bothell, WA 98011-9511 USA
ShopMartingale.com

Printed in China
18 17 16 15 14 13   8 7 6 5 4 3 2 1

**Library of Congress Cataloging-in-Publication Data
is available upon request.**

ISBN: 978-1-60468-337-0

Mission Statement

Dedicated to providing quality products and service to inspire creativity.

CREDITS

PRESIDENT AND CEO: Tom Wierzbicki

EDITOR IN CHIEF: Mary V. Green

DESIGN DIRECTOR: Paula Schlosser

MANAGING EDITOR: Karen Costello Soltys

ACQUISITIONS EDITOR: Karen M. Burns

TECHNICAL EDITOR: Amy Polcyn

COPY EDITOR: Sheila Chapman Ryan

PRODUCTION MANAGER: Regina Girard

COVER AND INTERIOR DESIGNER: Adrienne Smitke

PHOTOGRAPHER: Brent Kane

ILLUSTRATOR: Cheryl Fall

Contents

FOREWORD

Pink is the assigned color for breast-cancer awareness. We all know of the pink ribbons and pink fundraisers for the cause. I'm guessing that pink was chosen because it's the traditional color for girls in the United States, as well as being a very feminine color. Pink is also associated with a stylish fashion doll, a popular makeup company, a couple of movies, bands and songs, a line of lingerie, and a famous cartoon panther. Pink is meant to be a symbol of support—but not to stereotype women, especially women with breast cancer.

This book is not intended to pigeonhole anyone. It's meant to acknowledge the color pink as the color of hope for breast-cancer awareness and for finding a cure. It's a pretty color with infinite shades and hues that look even prettier when gathered together in one book. There are many organizations that accept donations for breast-cancer research and also many ways to donate one's time or knitting skills. Rather than choosing for you, I recommend you seek out local places—give in your own way and to the organization of your choice.

Introduction

Knitters are doers. We like to plan projects and touch yarn. We transform yarn into something to use or to wear. While we're enjoying the feel of the fibers through our hands and watching the fabric we create from a "piece of string," we're thinking about the people who will use or wear this item. We hope that they love it! We may be nervous about whether they'll like the colors or pattern we've chosen or whether they'll take the time to hand wash the item. But at the end of the day or month we have something tangible to show for our time. We've used our time to make beautiful and thoughtful gifts for others. We can teach others how to knit, we can pray or send healing thoughts while we knit, we can build friendships while we knit, we can knit for charities, and we can knit for ourselves. Our knitting can make a long wait seem short, and can even open conversations with strangers.

A pink ribbon signifies the fight against breast cancer. Breast cancer is an ugly, frightening enemy. According to the National Breast Cancer Foundation, one in eight women will be diagnosed with breast cancer. Someone you know has most likely battled it. It's the most common cancer in women worldwide and the second leading cause of death in women. The ribbon reminds us that we are *fighting* breast cancer—giving a part of ourselves to help win the battle. We walk and run for the cause. We wear the pink ribbon for the cause. We donate money to the cause.

What else can we do? We can learn about breast health, including self examinations and mammograms. For a few years, my girlfriend and I scheduled our mammos on Valentine's Day, then went to lunch afterward. It held us accountable each year, helped us remember the date, and made the day enjoyable too.

This book is meant to bring together the pink symbol of breast-cancer awareness and knitting. The projects are shown in a wide variety of pinks, not just the sweet, feminine pink shown on the awareness ribbon. Pink brings these designs together and makes them all prettier, yet they're each a unique shade of pink. This book provides you many projects and ideas to use in your own way. The designs are quick, practical, and fun, and most will fit anyone. Of course, not everyone loves pink. Substitute any color you like (see "Choosing Yarns" on page 73 for information on substituting fibers). For other cancer-awareness colors of hope, see the chart at right.

As you look through the pages of this book, think about the recipient of your knitting: a friend, a family member, yourself, or maybe a charity? I recommend knitting locally just as I like to shop locally. Ask your local yarn shop about charity knitting clubs. Contact your local hospital's cancer or chemo center about knitting for patients. Consider offering knitting lessons to someone going through chemo. Find your nearest branch of the American Cancer Society; they offer classes and free gifts to cancer patients and could use your help or donations.

CANCER-AWARENESS COLORS	
All cancer survivors	Lavender
Bladder cancer	Yellow
Bone cancer	White with gold outline
Brain cancer	Gray
Breast cancer	Pink
Childhood cancer	Gold
Colon and colorectal cancer	Brown
Esophageal cancer	Periwinkle blue
Gynecological cancer	Lavender
Head and neck cancer	Red with white stripe
Hodgkin's disease	Violet
Hospice care	Burgundy
Kidney/renal cancer	Kelly green
Leiomyosarcoma	Purple
Leukemia	Orange
Lung cancer	Pearl
Lymphoma	Red
Male breast cancer	Half blue and half pink
Melanoma	Black
Mesothelioma	Royal blue
Multiple myeloma	Burgundy
Ovarian cancer	Teal
Pancreatic cancer	Purple
Prostate cancer	Light blue
Retinoblastoma	White
Testicular cancer	Orchid/violet
Thyroid cancer	Light blue
Transplant	Green

Gentle Caress Cowl

Wrap this soft cowl twice around your neck for a thick cozy bundling, or let it drape loosely once around your neck like a necklace.

SKILL LEVEL: Easy

FINISHED MEASUREMENTS:
35" circumference x 7" wide

MATERIALS

1 hank of Worsted Merino Superwash by Plymouth Yarn Company Inc. (100% superwash fine merino wool; 100 g; 218 yds) in color 48

Size 7 (4.5 mm) 24" circular needle or size required to obtain gauge

Stitch markers

Tapestry needle

GAUGE

16 sts and 30 rows = 4" in diagonal lace patt

DIAGONAL LACE PATTERN

(Multiple of 6 sts)

Rnd 1: *Ssk, K2, YO, K2; rep from * around.

Rnd 2: Knit.

Rep rnds 1 and 2 for patt.

COWL

CO 138 sts. Place marker for beg of rnd. Join, being careful not to twist sts. Work in diagonal lace patt for 7". BO loosely.

FINISHING

Weave in ends. Block.

Diagonal lace

						2
		O			/	1

6-st repeat
Work all rnds from right to left.

Key

O	YO
◺	Ssk
☐	K

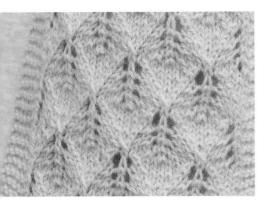

Small Blessings Scarf

Who wouldn't feel loved with baby alpaca and angora wrapped around her? This beautiful lace is fun to knit and warm to wear.

SKILL LEVEL: Easy

FINISHED MEASUREMENTS:

7½" x 56" after blocking

MATERIALS

2 hanks of Fresco by Classic Elite Yarns (60% wool, 30% baby alpaca, 10% angora; 50 g; 162 yds) in color 5319

Size 5 (3.75 mm) needles or size required to obtain gauge

Tapestry needle

GAUGE

22 sts and 32 rows = 4" in candlelight lace patt after blocking

CANDLELIGHT LACE PATTERN

(Multiple of 10 + 1 sts)

Row 1 (RS): *K3, K2tog, YO, K1, YO, ssk, K2; rep from * to last st, K1.

Row 2 and all even-numbered rows: Purl.

Row 3: *K2, K2tog, K1, YO, K1, YO, K1, ssk, K1; rep from * to last st, K1.

Row 5: *K1, K2tog, K2, YO, K1, YO, K2, ssk; rep from * to last st, K1.

Row 7: K2tog, K3, YO, K1, YO, K3, *sl 1, K2tog, psso, K3, YO, K1, YO, K3; rep from * to last 2 sts, ssk.

Row 9: *K1, YO, ssk, K5, K2tog, YO; rep from * to last st, K1.

Row 11: *K1, YO, K1, ssk, K3, K2tog, K1, YO; rep from * to last st, K1.

Row 13: *K1, YO, K2, ssk, K1, K2tog, K2, YO; rep from * to last st, K1.

Row 15: *K1, YO, K3, sl 1, K2tog, psso, K3, YO; rep from * to last st, K1.

Row 16: Purl.

Rep rows 1–16 for patt.

SCARF

CO 41 sts. Knit 10 rows (5 ridges).

Row 1 (RS): K5, work row 1 of candlelight lace patt, K5.

Row 2: K5, work row 2 of candlelight lace patt, K5.

Rep rows 1 and 2. Continue in patt as set, working each subsequent row of lace patt until scarf measures approx 55" long, ending after row 8 or row 16. Knit 10 rows. BO.

FINISHING

Weave in ends. Block.

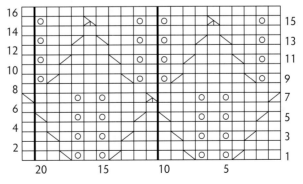

Candlelight lace

Key

⊠ Sl 1, K2tog, psso

◣ K2tog

◿ Ssk

⊡ YO

☐ K on RS, P on WS

10-st repeat + 1

Note: For row 7 work first 10 sts of chart for first repeat, repeat 10 outlined stitches across, ending last repeat with last st of chart.

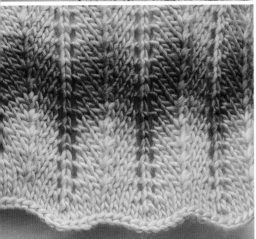

> ⫸ *What you do today is important because you're exchanging a day of your life for it.*
>
> *~Unknown*

Easy lace

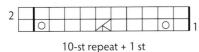

10-st repeat + 1 st

Key

◪ K3tog

□ YO

☐ K on RS, P on WS

Graceful Scarf

Don't let the gorgeous chevrons and color changes fool you—this scarf couldn't be easier. There's only one pattern row for the lace! Every right-side row is the same. The incredible hand-dyed yarn adds the stripes.

SKILL LEVEL: Easy

FINISHED MEASUREMENTS: 7½" x 56"

MATERIALS

2 skeins of Migrations by Alchemy Yarns of Transformation (30% silk, 70% wool; 50 g; 170 yds) in color 203mig Rosy Finch

Size 7 (4.5 mm) needles or size required to obtain gauge

Tapestry needle

GAUGE

24 sts and 28 rows = 4" in easy lace patt after blocking

EASY LACE PATTERN

(Multiple of 10 + 1 sts)

Row 1 (RS): *K1, YO, K3, K3tog, K3, YO; rep from * to last st, K1.

Row 2: Purl.

Rep rows 1 and 2 for patt.

SCARF

CO 45 sts.

Edging

Row 1 (RS): K2, pm, knit to last 2 sts, pm, move yarn to front, sl 2 pw.

Row 2: K2, sl marker, purl to last 2 sts, sl marker, leave yarn in front, sl 2 pw.

Begin Lace

Row 1 (RS): K2, sl marker, *K1, YO, K3, K3tog, K3, YO; rep from * to last 3 sts, K1, sl marker, move yarn to front, sl 2 pw.

Row 2: K2, sl marker, purl to last 2 sts, sl marker, leave yarn in front, sl 2 pw.

Rep these 2 rows until scarf measures 56" unstretched, ending after WS row.

Work rows 1 and 2 of edging patt.

BO loosely.

FINISHING

Weave in ends. Block.

Feeling Lovely Scarf

Feminine glamour at its best is simple and classy. This scarf is very easy and the yarn does all the work.

SKILL LEVEL: Beginner
FINISHED MEASUREMENTS:
6" x 56"

MATERIALS

2 skeins of Soft Payette by Rozetti Yarn (70% acrylic, 22% polyester, 8% soft Payette; 100 g; 224 yds) in color 158-03 Rose Quartz (**3**

Size 6 (4 mm) needles or size required to obtain gauge

Tapestry needle

GAUGE

18 sts and 24 rows = 4" in broken rib patt

BROKEN RIB PATTERN

(Multiple of 2 + 1 sts)

Row 1 (RS): Knit.

Row 2: P1, *K1, P1; rep from * across.

Rep rows 1 and 2 for patt.

SCARF

CO 27 sts. Work in broken rib patt until scarf measures 56". BO.

FINISHING

Weave in ends. Block.

Broken rib

(Odd number of sts)

Key

☐ K on RS, P on WS

▣ P on RS, K on WS

I  You Pillow

Pillows are soft and comforting. This one is compact, portable, and says, "I love you!"

SKILL LEVEL: Beginner

FINISHED MEASUREMENTS:
12" x 12"

MATERIALS

1 ball of Petals Socks by Debbie Macomber Blossom Street Collection (50% fine merino superwash wool, 20% angora, 30% nylon; 100 g; 462 yds) in color 601 Cherry Blossom

Size 4 (3.5 mm) straight and double-pointed needles or size required to obtain gauge

Square pillow form, 12" x 12"

Tapestry needle

GAUGE

24 sts and 32 rows = 4" in St st

PILLOW

CO 72 sts. Work in St st for 12", ending after a RS row. Knit next WS row. Knit next RS row and then cont in St st for 12". BO.

FINISHING

Fold along purl ridge. Sew 2 sides, leaving 1 side open. Insert pillow form. Sew final side closed.

I-CORD EMBELLISHMENTS

With double-pointed needles, CO 4 sts. Work in I-cord (see page 75) for 48". BO. Sew I-cord to edges of pillow. Make another I-cord, 30" long. Arrange on pillow to make a heart. Sew in place.

> *I've seen better days, but I've also seen worse. I don't have everything I want, but I do have all I need. I woke up with some aches and pains, but I woke up. My life may not be perfect, but I'm blessed.*
>
> *~Unknown*

Cuddle Me Bolster Pillow

A bolster pillow is comfortable and surprisingly easy to make. The body of the pillow is a rectangle, and the ends are each knit the same way as the crown of a hat.

SKILL LEVEL: Easy

FINISHED MEASUREMENTS:

14" long x 7" diameter

MATERIALS

Nature Spun Chunky by Brown Sheep Company, Inc. (100% wool; 200 g; 155 yds) **5**

MC: 1 skein in color N85 Peruvian Pink

CC: 1 skein in color N87 Victorian Pink

Size 10 (6 mm) straight and double-pointed needles or size required to obtain gauge

Bolster pillow form, 16" long x 5" diameter

Tapestry needle

GAUGE

15 sts and 22 rows = 4" in striped basket weave patt

STRIPED BASKET WEAVE PATTERN

(Multiple of 6 sts)

Row 1 (RS): With MC, knit.

Row 2: With MC, purl.

Rows 3 and 5: With MC, *K1, P4, K1; rep from * across.

Rows 4 and 6: With MC, *P1, K4, P1; rep from * across.

Row 7: With CC, knit.

Row 8: With CC, purl.

Rows 9 and 11: With CC, *P2, K2, P2; rep from * across.

Rows 10 and 12: With CC, *K2, P2, K2; rep from * across.

Rep rows 1–12 for patt.

PILLOW TUBE

With straight needles and MC, CO 60 sts. Work in striped basket weave patt until piece measures 14", ending after row 6. Do not BO or cut yarn. Thread sts onto scrap yarn.

FINISHING

Sew sides tog to make tube, leaving 6" open in center.

With double-pointed needles and MC, PU 60 sts from CO edge. Pm for beg of rnd.

Rnd 1: *K8; K2tog; rep from * around—54 sts.

Rnd 2 and all even-numbered rnds: Knit.

Rnd 3: *K7; K2tog; rep from * around—48 sts.

Rnd 5: *K6; K2tog; rep from * around—42 sts.

Rnd 7: *K5; K2tog; rep from * around—36 sts.

Rnd 9: *K4; K2tog; rep from * around—30 sts.

Rnd 11: *K3; K2tog; rep from * around—24 sts.

Rnd 13: *K2; K2tog; rep from * around—18 sts.

Rnd 15: *K1, K2tog; rep from * around—12 sts.

Rnd 17: K2tog around—6 sts. Cut yarn. Thread through rem sts. Fasten off.

Replace sts from other end to needles. Knit 1 rnd. Work rnds 1–17 same as for first end.

Insert pillow form through side opening. Finish sewing seam.

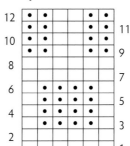

Striped basket weave

6-st repeat

Key

⊡ P on RS, K on WS

☐ K on RS, P on WS

Work rows 1-6 in MC; rows 7-12 in CC.

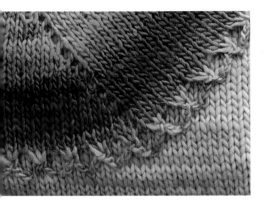

Main Squeeze Pillow

Beautiful hand-dyed colors radiate from the center of this pillow. The variegated yarn colors do all the pattern work, leaving nothing but fun knitting to do!

SKILL LEVEL: Intermediate

FINISHED MEASUREMENTS:

16" x 16"

MATERIALS

MC: 2 skeins of Worsted by Freia Fine Handpaint Yarns (100% wool; 50 g; 85 yds) in color Bell Heather (4)

CC: 1 skein of Sport by Freia Fine Handpaint Yarns (100% wool; 50 g; 145 yds) in color Tapestry (3)

Size 8 (5 mm) needles or size required to obtain gauge

Size 6 (4 mm) double-pointed and 16" circular needles

Size G-6 (4 mm) crochet hook

Square pillow form, 16" x 16"

Stitch marker

Tapestry needle

GAUGE

16 sts and 22 rows = 4" in St st using larger needles and MC

PILLOW

With larger needles and MC, CO 64 sts. Work in St st until pillow measures 32". BO.

Fold in half and sew 2 sides; leave 1 side open for stuffing.

CIRCLE

With double-pointed needles and CC, CO 8 sts. Pm and join, being careful not to twist the sts.

Rnd 1 and all odd-numbered rnds: Knit.

Rnd 2: *YO, K1; rep from * around—16 sts.

Rnd 4: *YO, K2; rep from * around—24 sts.

Rnd 6: *YO, K3; rep from * around—32 sts.

Rnd 8: *YO, K4; rep from * around—40 sts.

Rnd 10: *YO, K5; rep from * around—48 sts.

Rnd 12: *YO, K6; rep from * around—56 sts.

Rnd 14: *YO, K7; rep from * around—64 sts.

Rnd 16: *YO, K8; rep from * around—72 sts.

Rnd 18: *YO, K9; rep from * around—80 sts.

Rnd 20: *YO, K10; rep from * around—88 sts.

Rnd 22: *YO, K11; rep from * around—96 sts.

Rnd 24: *YO, K12; rep from * around—104 sts.

Rnd 26: *YO, K13; rep from * around—112 sts.

Rnd 28: *YO, K14; rep from * around—120 sts.

Rnd 30: *YO, K15; rep from * around—128 sts.

Rnd 32: *YO, K16; rep from * around—136 sts.

Rnd 34: *YO, K17; rep from * around—144 sts.

Rnd 36: *YO, K18; rep from * around—152 sts.

Next rnd: BO as follows: With crochet hook, *insert hook into 3 sts on LH needle as if to K3tog tbl, YO, pull loop through, chain 5; rep from * around. Fasten off. Weave in ends. Block circle. Sew circle to front of pillow.

FINISHING

Insert pillow form into pillow. Sew last side closed. Weave in ends.

Pretty Adornment Hat

Angora is one of the softest, warmest fibers to be found. It would be comfortable as a chemo hat, during which scalps can be overly sensitive to touch. Of course, it would be a treat for anyone else too!

SKILL LEVEL: Easy

FINISHED MEASUREMENTS: 20" circumference

MATERIALS

4 skeins of Angora Glitz by Plymouth Yarn Company Inc. (96% angora, 2% metallic, 2% nylon; 10 g; 49 yds) in color 712 pink/silver

Size 8 (5 mm) 16" circular and double-pointed needles or size required to obtain gauge

Stitch marker

Tapestry needle

GAUGE

16 sts and 18 rows = 4" in garter st

14 sts and 36 rows = 4" in brioche st patt

BRIOCHE STITCH PATTERN

(Even number of sts)

Rnd 1: *K1, P1; rep from * around.

Rnd 2: *K1b, K1; rep from * around.

Rep rnds 1 and 2 for patt.

HAT

With circular needle, CO 80 sts. Pm and join, being careful not to twist the sts.

*Purl 1 rnd, knit 1 rnd; rep from * for a total of 10 rnds.

Work in brioche st patt until hat measures 9" from beg, ending after rnd 2.

SHAPE CROWN

Cont with circular needle; change to double-pointed needles when needed.

Rnd 1: *(K1, P1) 4 times, K1, S2KP, (K1, P1) 4 times; rep from * around—72 sts.

Rnd 2: *K1b, K1; rep from * around.

Rnd 3: *(K1, P1) 4 times, S2KP, (P1, K1) 3 times, P1; rep from * around—64 sts.

Rnd 4: *(K1b, K1) 4 times, K2, (K1b, K1) 3 times; rep from * around.

Rnd 5: *(K1, P1) 3 times, K1, S2KP, (K1, P1) 3 times; rep from * around—56 sts.

Rnd 6: *K1b, K1; rep from * around.

Rnd 7: *(K1, P1) 3 times, S2KP, (P1, K1) 2 times, P1; rep from * around—48 sts.

Rnd 8: *(K1b, K1) 3 times, K2, (K1b, K1) 2 times; rep from * around.

Rnd 9: *(K1, P1) 2 times, K1, S2KP, (K1, P1) 2 times; rep from * around—40 sts.

Rnd 10: *K1b, K1; rep from * around.

Rnd 11: *(K1, P1) 2 times, S2KP, P1, K1, P1; rep from * around—32 sts.

Rnd 12: *(K1b, K1) 2 times, K2, K1b, K1; rep from * around.

Rnd 13: *K1, P1, K1, S2KP, K1, P1; rep from * around—24 sts.

Rnd 14: *K1b, K1; rep from * around.

Rnd 15: *K1, P1, S2KP, P1; rep from * around—16 sts.

Cut yarn. Thread through rem sts. Fasten off.

FINISHING

Weave in ends. Block.

Entwined Hat

Instead of a typical cast-on edge, this hat begins as a headband that's worked sideways around *the head. The remainder of the project is picked up and knit from the headband, making for a hat that's nonbinding and comfortable—not to mention cute!*

SKILL LEVEL: Intermediate

FINISHED MEASUREMENTS:

22" circumference

MATERIALS

1 skein of Tatamy by Kraemer Yarns (45% cotton, 55% acrylic; 100 g; 250 yds) in color It's a Girl

Size 6 (4 mm) 16" circular and double-pointed needles or size required to obtain gauge

Cable needle

Stitch marker

Tapestry needle

GAUGE

22 sts and 28 rows = 4" in garter st

CABLE PATTERN

(Multiple of 8 sts)

Row 1 and all odd-numbered rows (WS): Purl. (When working in the round, knit.)

Rows 2, 4, and 6: Knit.

Row 8: Sl 4 sts to cn, hold in front, K4, K4 from cn.

Rep rows 1–8 for patt.

HAT

With band back and forth; then work rest of hat in the round.

Horizontal Hat Band

With circular needle, CO 16 sts. K4, cable patt over next 8 sts, K4. Work rows 1–8 of cable patt until band measures 21" when slightly stretched, ending after row 8. BO. Sew CO edge to BO edge.

Hat Body

PU 120 sts around one edge of band. Pm and join.

Rnd 1: Knit.

Rnd 2: *P22, work cable patt over next 8 sts; rep from * around.

Rep these 2 rnds until hat measures 6" from lower edge of band.

Shape Crown

Cont with circular needle; change to double-pointed needles when needed.

Rnd 1: *K2tog, K18, ssk, work cable patt over next 8 sts; rep from * around—112 sts.

Rnd 2: *P20, work cable patt over next 8 sts; rep from * around.

Rnd 3: *K2tog, K16, ssk, work cable patt over next 8 sts; rep from * around—104 sts.

Rnd 4: *P18, work cable patt over next 8 sts; rep from * around.

Rnd 5: *K2tog, K14, ssk, work cable patt over next 8 sts; rep from * around—96 sts.

Rnd 6: *K16, work cable patt over next 8 sts; rep from * around.

Rnd 7: *K2tog, K12, ssk, work cable patt over next 8 sts; rep from * around—88 sts.

Rnd 8: *P14, work cable patt over next 8 sts; rep from * around.

Rnd 9: *K2tog, K10, ssk, work cable patt over next 8 sts; rep from * around—80 sts.

Rnd 10: *P12, work cable patt over next 8 sts; rep from * around.

Rnd 11: *K2tog, K8, ssk, work cable patt over next 8 sts; rep from * around—72 sts.

Rnd 12: *P10, work cable patt over next 8 sts; rep from * around.

Rnd 13: *K2tog, K6, ssk, work cable patt over next 8 sts; rep from * around—64 sts.

Rnd 14: *P8, work cable patt over next 8 sts; rep from * around.

Rnd 15: *K2tog, K4, ssk, work cable patt over next 8 sts; rep from * around—56 sts.

Rnd 16: *P6, work cable patt over next 8 sts; rep from * around.

Rnd 17: *K2tog, K2, ssk, work cable patt over next 8 sts; rep from * around—48 sts.

Rnd 18: *P4, work cable patt over next 8 sts; rep from * around.

Rnd 19: *K2tog, ssk, work cable patt over next 8 sts; rep from * around—40 sts.

Rnd 20: *P2, work cable patt over next 8 sts; rep from * around.

Rnd 21: *K2tog, (ssk) twice, (K2tog) twice; rep from * around—20 sts.

Cut yarn. Thread through rem sts. Fasten off.

FINISHING

Weave in ends. Block.

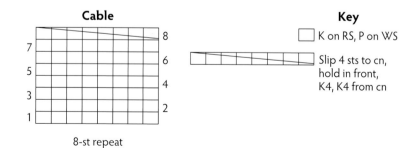

Cable

8-st repeat

Key

☐ K on RS, P on WS

Slip 4 sts to cn, hold in front, K4, K4 from cn

My *Indoor* Chemo Hat

The shell edging on this hat has just a hint of a scallop, and blends into faux cables for a soft, pretty look. The yarn is a superfine nylon-acrylic blend with lots of stretch.

By Janet Rehfeldt, author of Crochet Pink (Martingale, 2013)

SKILL LEVEL: Intermediate

SIZES: Medium (Large)

FINISHED MEASUREMENTS:

18½" circumference, unstretched*

Due to stretch of yarn and the lace technique used, hat will fit from 16" to 25" circumference if cast on is done loosely but not sloppily. Allowance is made in height from base to crown for large size.

MATERIALS

1 skein of Comfort DK by Berroco, Inc. (50% superfine nylon, 50% superfine acrylic; 50 g; 178 yds) in color 2843 Kittens

Size 5 (3.75 mm) 16" circular and double-pointed needles or size required to obtain gauge

Stitch marker

Tapestry needle

GAUGE

25 sts and 38 rnds = 4" in St st

EDGING

With circular needle, loosely CO 108 sts. Pm and join, being careful not to twist the sts. For hat without edging, skip to rnd 1 of body.

Rnd 1: *K1, YO, K2, sl 1, K2tog, psso, K2, YO, K1; rep from * around.

Rnd 2 and all even-numbered rnds: Knit.

Rnd 3: *K2, YO, K1, sl 1, K2tog, psso, K1, YO, K2; rep from * around.

Rnd 5: *K3, YO, sl 1, K2tog, psso, YO, K3; rep from * around.

Rnd 7: *K3, YO, ssk, K4; rep from * around.

Rnd 8: Knit.

Rep rnds 1–8 once (twice) more; on rnd 8, knit YOs through the back, twisting to close hole.

BODY OF HAT

Knit 1 rnd, inc 4 sts spaced evenly—112 sts.

Rnds 1 and 2: *K6, P2; rep from * around.

Rnd 3: *YO, K2, ssk, K2, P2; rep from * around.

Rnd 4: Rep rnd 1.

Rnd 5: *K1, YO, K2, ssk, K1, P2; rep from * around.

Rnd 6: Rep rnd 1.

Rnd 7: *K2, YO, K2, ssk, P2; rep from * around.

Rnds 8–10: Rep rnd 1.

Rnd 11: *K2, K2tog, K2, YO, P2; rep from * around.

Rnd 12: Rep rnd 1.

Rnd 13: *K1, K2tog, K2, YO, K1, P2; rep from * around.

Rnd 14: Rep rnd 1.

Rnd 15: *K2tog, K2, YO, K2, P2; rep from * around.

Rnd 16: Rep rnd 1.

Rep rnds 1–16 until hat measures 6 (7¼)" from bottom edge, ending after rnd 8 or 16.

SHAPE CROWN

Cont with circular needle; change to double-pointed needles when needed.

Rnd 1: Knit, dec 2 sts evenly—110 sts.

Rnd 2: *K20, ssk, rep from * around—105 sts.

Rnd 3 and all odd-numbered rnds: Knit.

Rnd 4: *K19, ssk; rep from * around—100 sts.

Rnd 6: *K18, ssk; rep from * around—95 sts.

Rnd 8: *K17, ssk; rep from * around—90 sts.

Rnds 9–27: Rep rnds 3 and 4, working 1 less st between decs every other rnd as established—45 sts.

Next rnd: *K1, ssk; rep from * around—30 sts.

Next rnd: Knit.

Next rnd: *K1, ssk; rep from * around—20 sts.

Cut yarn, leaving 6" tail. Thread through rem sts. Fasten off.

FINISHING

Weave in ends. Block.

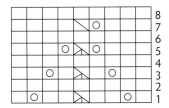

Hat edging

8
7
6
5
4
3
2
1

9-st repeat
Work all rnds from right to left.

Hat body

16
15
14
13
12
11
10
9
8
7
6
5
4
3
2
1

8-st repeat
Work all rnds from right to left.

Key

K2tog

Sl 1, K2tog, psso

Ssk

YO

P

K

Hearty Hands Mittens

Mittens have a childlike sense of fun, so using bright colors makes them all the more warm and cheerful.

SKILL LEVEL: Intermediate

FINISHED MEASUREMENTS:
8" circumference x approx 9" from cuff to fingertip

MATERIALS

1 skein of Shepherd Worsted by Lorna's Laces (100% superwash wool; 113 g; 225 yds) in color 307 Tickled Pink

Size 8 (5 mm) double-pointed needles or size required to obtain gauge

Stitch marker

Tapestry needle

GAUGE

18 sts and 24 rnds = 4" in St st

2 X 2 RIBBING PATTERN

(Multiple of 4 sts)

All rnds: *K2, P2; rep from * around.

CUFF

CO 36 sts. Pm and join, being careful not to twist the sts. Work in 2 x 2 ribbing patt for 2". Knit 2 rnds even.

THUMB GUSSET

Rnd 1: (Kfb) twice, knit around—38 sts.

Rnds 2 and 3: Knit.

Rnd 4: Kfb, K2, Kfb, knit around—40 sts.

Rnds 5 and 6: Knit.

Rnd 7: Kfb, K4, Kfb, knit around—42 sts.

Rnds 8 and 9: Knit.

Rnd 10: Kfb, K6, Kfb, knit around—44 sts.

Rnds 11 and 12: Knit.

Rnd 13: K1, K9 and place these 9 sts on scrap yarn for thumb, knit around, remove marker—35 sts.

HAND

Using cable CO, CO 2 sts, pm, CO 3 sts, knit to marker—40 sts. Knit every rnd until hand measures 3½" from thumb opening or 1½" less than desired length from thumb opening to fingertip.

SHAPE TOP

Rnd 1: *K3, K2tog; rep from * around—32 sts.

Rnds 2 and 3: Knit.

Rnd 4: *K2, K2tog; rep from * around—24 sts.

Rnds 5 and 6: Knit.

Rnd 7: *K1, K2tog; rep from * around—16 sts.

Rnds 8 and 9: Knit.

Rnd 10: *K2tog; rep from * around—8 sts.

Cut yarn. Thread through rem sts. Fasten off.

THUMB

PU 5 sts from CO sts above thumb opening, knit 9 sts from holder—14 sts. Pm for beg of rnd.

Knit every rnd until thumb measures 2".

Next rnd: *K2tog; rep from * around—7 sts.

Cut yarn. Thread through rem sts. Fasten off.

FINISHING

Weave in ends.

Scars may heal, blood counts may normalize, years may pass. But never again will the simple act of waking up to a normal, boring day as a healthy individual be taken for granted, nor go unappreciated.

~Unknown

Delicious Fingerless Gloves

The cuff is knit from side to side using garter-stitch short rows. This makes for comfy, stretchy cuffs with a slight feminine ruffle, without the fussiness of lace.

SKILL LEVEL: Intermediate
FINISHED MEASUREMENTS:
7½" circumference x 8" long

MATERIALS

2 skeins of Scrumptious by Kollage Yarns (70% angora, 30% silk; 35 g; 100 yds) in color 6812 Strawberry Pie

Size 7 (4.5 mm) double-pointed needles or size required to obtain gauge

Stitch marker

Tapestry needle

GAUGE

20 sts and 28 rows = 4" in St st

CUFF

CO 10 sts.

Row 1 (RS): K10.

Row 2: K4, turn.

Row 3: K4.

Row 4: K10.

Rep rows 1–4 until short edge measures 6".

BO.

Sew CO edge to BO edge.

LOWER HAND

Beg at seam, PU 33 sts evenly spaced around shorter edge of cuff. Pm for beg of rnd. Knit every rnd until glove measures 3".

SHAPE THUMB GUSSET

Rnd 1: K1, M1, K32, M1—35 sts.

Rnds 2 and 3: Knit.

Rnd 4: K2, M1, K32, M1, K1— 37 sts.

Rnds 5 and 6: Knit.

Rnd 7: K3, M1, K32, M1, K2—39 sts.

Rnds 8 and 9: Knit.

Rnd 10: K4, M1, K32, M1, K3—41 sts.

Rnds 11 and 12: Knit.

Rnd 13: K5, M1, K32, M1, K4—43 sts.

Rnds 14 and 15: Knit.

Rnd 16: K6, M1, K32, M1, K5—45 sts.

Rnds 17 and 18: Knit.

Rnd 19: K7, M1, K32, M1, K6—47 sts.

Rnd 20: K8, sl 8 sts just worked to scrap yarn, K32, sl rem 7 sts to scrap yarn.

UPPER HAND

Working only on hand sts, CO 5 sts above thumb—37 sts. Knit every rnd for 2". BO.

THUMB

PU 4 sts from edge of CO above thumb, knit around 15 sts from holder—19 sts.

Dec rnd: K1, (K2tog) twice, knit to last st of rnd, K2tog last st and first st of next rnd—16 sts.

Knit every rnd for 1½".

BO.

FINISHING

Weave in ends.

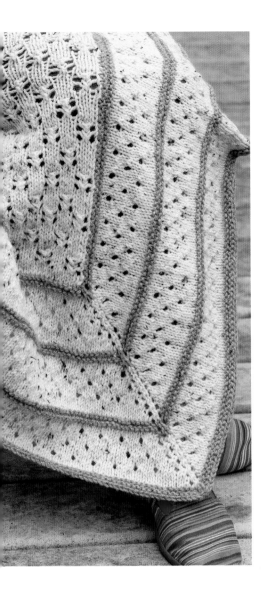

Wrapped in Warmth Blanket

The center panel is knit first, and then framed with mitered-corner borders. Varied yet simple stitch patterns make this fun and interesting to knit.

SKILL LEVEL: Easy

FINISHED MEASUREMENTS:
35" x 45"

MATERIALS

MC: 5 skeins of Encore Tweed by Plymouth Yarn Company Inc. (75% acrylic, 22% wool, 3% rayon; 100 g; 200 yds) in color 5539

CC: 1 skein of Encore Worsted by Plymouth Yarn Company Inc. (75% acrylic, 25% wool; 100 g; 200 yds) in color 194 (4)

Size 8 (5 mm) needles or size required to obtain gauge

Stitch markers: 3 the same and 1 unique

Tapestry needle

GAUGE

15 sts and 23 rows = 4" in St st

CHECKED LACE PATTERN

(Multiple of 6 + 5 sts)

Rows 1 and 3 (RS): K1, *YO, sl 1, K2tog, psso, YO, K3; rep from * to last 4 sts, YO, sl 1, K2tog, psso, YO, K1.

Row 2 and all even-numbered rows: Purl.

Row 5: Knit.

Rows 7 and 9: K1, *K3, YO, sl 1, K2tog, psso, YO; rep from * across to last 4 sts, K4.

Row 11: Knit.

Row 12: Purl.

Rep rows 1–12 for patt.

THROW

Throw begins in the center. After knitting the lace rectangle, stitches are picked up and knit around the perimeter of the rectangle, inc at each corner every other rnd.

With MC, CO 59 sts. Work in checked lace patt for 25", ending after row 6 or 12. Cut MC. Do not BO.

BORDER

Join CC.

Rnd 1: Knit across 59 sts, pm for corner, PU 95 sts along side, pm for corner, PU 59 sts from CO edge, pm for corner, PU 95 sts along side, place unique marker for beg of rnd.

Rnd 2: *K1, purl to marker; rep from * around.

Rnd 3: *K1, YO, knit to marker, YO, sl marker; rep from * around—60-96-60-96 sts per side plus 1 st at each corner.

Rnd 4: *K1, purl to marker; rep from * around.

Cut CC. Join MC.

Rnd 5: *K1, YO, knit to marker, YO, sl marker; rep from * around—62-98-62-98 sts per side plus 1 st at each corner.

Rnd 6: Knit.

Rnd 7: *K1, YO, knit to marker, YO, sl marker; rep from * around—64-100-64-100 sts per side plus 1 st at each corner.

Rnd 8: *K1, (K2, YO, K2tog) to next marker; rep from * around.

Rnd 9: *K1, YO, knit to marker, YO, sl marker; rep from * around—66-102-66-102 sts per side plus 1 st at each corner.

Rnd 10: Knit.

Rnd 11: *K1, YO, knit to marker, YO, sl marker; rep from * around—68-104-68-104 sts per side plus 1 st at each corner.

Rnd 12: *K1, (K2, YO, K2tog) to next marker; rep from * around.

Rnd 13: *K1, YO, knit to marker, YO, sl marker; rep from * around—70-106-70-106 sts per side plus 1 st at each corner.

Rnd 14: Knit.

Rnd 15: *K1, YO, knit to marker, YO, sl marker; rep from * around—72-108-72-108 sts per side plus 1 st at each corner.

Rnd 16: *K1, (K2, YO, K2tog) to next marker; rep from * around.

Rnd 17: *K1, YO, knit to marker, YO, sl marker; rep from * around—74-110-74-110 sts per side plus 1 st at each corner.

Rnd 18: Knit.

Rnd 19: *K1, YO, knit to marker, YO, sl marker; rep from * around—76-112-76-112 sts per side plus 1 st at each corner.

Rnd 20: Knit.

Do not cut MC; carry it loosely until needed. Join CC.

Rnd 21: *K1, YO, knit to marker, YO, sl marker; rep from * around—78-114-78-114 sts per side plus 1 st at each corner.

Rnd 22: *K1, purl to marker; rep from * around.

Rnd 23: *K1, YO, knit to marker, YO, sl marker; rep from * around—80-116-80-116 sts per side plus 1 st at each corner.

Rnd 24: *K1, purl to marker; rep from * around.

Cut CC.

Rnd 25: With MC, *K1, YO, knit to marker, YO, sl marker; rep from * around—82-118-82-118 sts per side plus 1 st at each corner.

Rnd 26: Knit.

Rnd 27: *K1, YO, knit to marker, YO, sl marker; rep from * around—84-120-84-120 sts per side plus 1 st at each corner.

Rnd 28: *K1, (K2, YO, K2tog) to next marker; rep from * around.

Rnd 29: *K1, YO, knit to marker, YO, sl marker; rep from * around—86-122-86-122 sts per side plus 1 st at each corner.

Rnd 30: Knit.

Rnd 31: *K1, YO, knit to marker, YO, sl marker; rep from * around—88-124-88-124 sts per side plus 1 st at each corner.

Rnd 32: *K1, (K2, YO, K2tog) to next marker; rep from * around.

Rnd 33: *K1, YO, knit to marker, YO, sl marker; rep from * around—90-126-90-126 sts per side plus 1 st at each corner.

Rnd 34: Knit.

Rnd 35: *K1, YO, knit to marker, YO, sl marker; rep from * around—92-128-92-128 sts per side plus 1 st at each corner.

Rnd 36: *K1, (K2, YO, K2tog) to next marker; rep from * around.

Rnd 37: *K1, YO, knit to marker, YO, sl marker; rep from * around—94-130-94-130 sts per side plus 1 st at each corner.

Rnd 38: Knit.

Rnd 39: *K1, YO, knit to marker, YO, sl marker; rep from * around—96-132-96-132 sts per side plus 1 st at each corner.

Rnd 40: Knit.

Do not cut MC; carry it loosely until needed. Join CC.

Rnd 41: *K1, YO, knit to marker, YO, sl marker; rep from * around—98-134-98-134 sts per side plus 1 st at each corner.

Rnd 42: *K1, purl to marker; rep from * around.

Rnd 43: *K1, YO, knit to marker, YO, sl marker; rep from * around—100-136-100-136 sts per side plus 1 st at each corner.

Rnd 44: *K1, purl to marker; rep from * around.

Cut CC.

Rnd 45: With MC, *K1, YO, knit to marker, YO, sl marker; rep from * around—102-138-102-138 sts per side plus 1 st at each corner.

Rnd 46: Knit.

Rnd 47: *K1, YO, knit to marker, YO, sl marker; rep from * around—104-140-104-140 sts per side plus 1 st at each corner.

Rnd 48: *K1, (K2, YO, K2tog) to next marker; rep from * around.

Rnd 49: *K1, YO, knit to marker, YO, sl marker; rep from * around—106-142-106-142 sts per side plus 1 st at each corner.

Rnd 50: Knit.

Rnd 51: *K1, YO, knit to marker, YO, sl marker; rep from * around—108-144-108-144 sts per side plus 1 st at each corner.

Rnd 52: *K1, (K2, YO, K2tog) to next marker; rep from * around.

Rnd 53: *K1, YO, knit to marker, YO, sl marker; rep from * around—110-146-110-146 sts per side plus 1 st at each corner.

Rnd 54: Knit.

Rnd 55: *K1, YO, knit to marker, YO, sl marker; rep from * around—112-148-112-148 sts per side plus 1 st at each corner.

Rnd 56: *K1, (K2, YO, K2tog) to next marker; rep from * around.

Rnd 57: *K1, YO, knit to marker, YO, sl marker; rep from * around—114-150-114-150 sts per side plus 1 st at each corner.

Rnd 58: Knit.

Rnd 59: *K1, YO, knit to marker, YO, sl marker; rep from * around—116-152-116-152 sts per side plus 1 st at each corner.

Rnd 60: Knit.

Cut MC. Join CC.

Rnd 61: *K1, YO, knit to marker, YO, sl marker; rep from * around—118-154-118-154 sts per side plus 1 st at each corner.

Rnd 62: *K1, purl to marker; rep from * around.

Rnd 63: *K1, YO, knit to marker, YO, sl marker; rep from * around—120-156-120-156 sts per side plus 1 st at each corner.

Rnd 64: *K1, purl to marker; rep from * around.

BO loosely.

FINISHING

Weave in ends. Block.

Comfort Lap Throw

This cozy blanket is small enough to take along in the car to appointments. The textured stitches look equally pretty from either side.

SKILL LEVEL: Beginner

FINISHED MEASUREMENTS:

36" x 36"

MATERIALS

6 hanks of Sweater by Spud and Chloë (55% wool, 45% organic cotton; 100 g; 160 yds) in color 7513

Size 7 (4.5 mm) needles or size required to obtain gauge

Tapestry needle

GAUGE

17 sts and 23 rows = 4" in diamonds patt after blocking

DIAMONDS PATTERN

(Multiple of 10 sts)

Row 1 (RS): *K5, P5; rep from * to end.

Row 2: *K5, P5; rep from * to end.

Row 3: *K5, P5; rep from * to end.

Row 4: *K5, P5; rep from * to end.

Row 5: *K4, P1, K1, P4; rep from * to end.

Row 6: *K4, P1, K1, P4; rep from * to end.

Row 7: *K3, P2, K2, P3; rep from * to end.

Row 8: *K3, P2, K2, P3; rep from * to end.

Row 9: *K2, P3, K3, P2; rep from * to end.

Row 10: *K2, P3, K3, P2; rep from * to end.

Row 11: *K1, P4, K4, P1; rep from * to end.

Row 12: *K1, P4, K4, P1; rep from * to end.

Row 13: *P5, K5; rep from * to end.

Row 14: *P5, K5; rep from * to end.

Row 15: *P5, K5; rep from * to end.

Row 16: *P5, K5; rep from * to end.

Row 17: *P4, K1, P1, K4; rep from * to end.

Row 18: *P4, K1, P1, K4; rep from * to end.

Row 19: *P3, K2, P2, K3; rep from * to end.

Row 20: *P3, K2, P2, K3; rep from * to end.

Row 21: *P2, K3, P3, K2; rep from * to end.

Row 22: *P2, K3, P3, K2; rep from * to end.

Row 23: *P1, K4, P4, K1; rep from * to end.

Row 24: *P1, K4, P4, K1; rep from * to end.

Rep rows 1–24 for patt.

FLAGS PATTERN

(Multiple of 13 sts)

Row 1 (RS): *K4, P1, K3, P1, K4; rep from * to end.

Row 2: *P3, K2, P3, K2, P3; rep from * to end.

Row 3: *K2, P3, K3, P3, K2; rep from * to end.

Row 4: *P1, K4, P3, K4, P1; rep from * to end.

Row 5: *P5, K3, P5; rep from * to end.

Row 6: *P1, K4, P3, K4, P1; rep from * to end.

Row 7: *K2, P3, K3, P3, K2; rep from * to end.

Row 8: *P3, K2, P3, K2, P3; rep from * to end.

Rows 9–24: Work rows 1–8 another 2 times.

Rep rows 1–24 for patt.

EDGE STITCHES

(Worked over 3 sts at each edge)

Every row: Wyif, sl 1, K2, work in patt to last 3 sts, K3.

THROW

CO 154 sts.

Knit 4 rows.

Next row (RS): Set up patt as follows:

Work 3 edge sts, pm, work flags patt over next 26 sts, pm, K3, work diamonds patt over next 90 sts, pm, K3, pm, work flags patt over next 26 sts, pm, 3 edge sts.

Work in set patt until blanket measures 36". Knit 4 rows. BO loosely.

FINISHING

Weave in ends. Block.

Diamonds

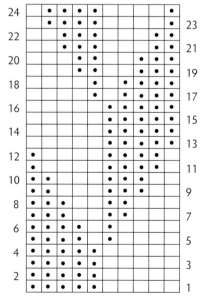

10-st repeat

Flags

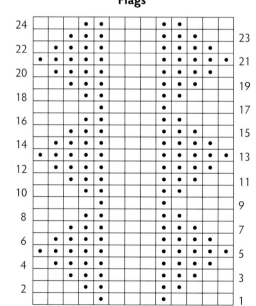

13-st repeat

Key

- P on RS, K on WS
- K on RS, P on WS

Handy Little Clutch

Whether it's makeup, knitting notions, or eyeglasses, we all have small items that need to be confined. This is a cute, quick clutch just for those items. Add a lining and zipper for true practicality.

SKILL LEVEL: Beginner

FINISHED MEASUREMENTS:
7" x 5"

MATERIALS

1 skein of Cotton Supreme Batik by Universal Yarn (100% cotton; 100 g; 180 yds) in color 28 Pink Lemonade

Size 7 (4.5 mm) needles or size required to obtain gauge

Tapestry needle

10" zipper

8" x 10" piece of cotton fabric for lining

8" x 10" piece of paper-backed fusible web

Iron

Sewing thread, needle, and pins

GAUGE

20 sts and 28 rows = 4" in textured triangles patt

TEXTURED TRIANGLES PATTERN

(Multiple of 12 sts)

Row 1 (RS): *K5, P1, K6; rep from * across.

Row 2: *P5, K3, P4; rep from * across.

Row 3: *K3, P5, K4; rep from * across.

Row 4: *P3, K7, P2; rep from * across.

Row 5: *K1, P9, K2; rep from * across.

Row 6: Purl.

Row 7: *P1, K11; rep from * across.

Row 8: *K1, P9, K2; rep from * across.

Row 9: *P3, K7, P2; rep from * across.

Row 10: *K3, P5, K4; rep from * across.

Row 11: *P5, K3, P4; rep from * across.

Row 12: Purl.

Rep rows 1–12 for patt.

BAG

CO 36 sts. Work in textured triangles patt for 10".

BO.

FINISHING

Lining

Cut fabric ½" larger than knitted piece on all sides.

Fold and press top and bottom edges under ½" for zipper edge of bag.

Fold lining in half with top and bottom edges aligned. Crease center fold line.

Cut away ½" of both side edges from 1 half of lining, from zippered edge to crease line. Fuse adhesive to wrong side of lining following package instructions. Trim to size. Allow to cool. Peel off paper. Align lining to wrong side of knit rectangle, with top and bottom aligned with cast-on and bind-off edges. The cut-away portion of side edges should align precisely with sides of knit rectangle, while other half extends ½"

beyond the knitted piece. Fuse in place, keeping iron away from side extensions. Sew side seams. Insert tip of iron into bag. Fuse extensions in place. Sew in zipper on top edge, leaving end sticking out and sewing extra length of zipper closed at top (see "Fused Lining" and "Zippers" on page 76).

Textured triangles

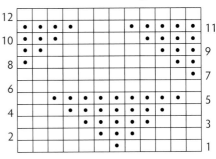

12-st repeat

Key

- • P on RS, K on WS
- ☐ K on RS, P on WS

Lining diagram

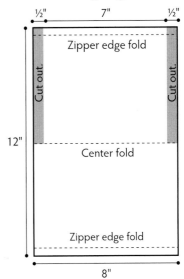

※ While in chemotherapy for breast cancer, one of my friends, who was probably sick of having me call weekly to whine about treatment side effects, told me I needed a hobby. I have since gotten serious about crocheting and later knitting. I have since become a yarn addict with a huge stash of yarn at home—some call me a lifetime member of SABLE (Stash Acquired Beyond Life Expectancy). My vacations have become traveling from yarn store to yarn store. Knitting and crocheting have given me a focus on something besides my health—I can create and make progress on something instead of thinking about recurrence and side effects. While I love to knit, I can barely follow a pattern—chemo brain makes it difficult to remember if I'm on the right side or the wrong side and to count stitches.

~Caroline,
www.carolinemfr.blogspot.com

Classy Felted Purse

A felted purse is sturdy and practical, but it can also be classy. This one uses a little hardware and a zipper, as well as a final "shave" to give it a sleek finished appearance.

SKILL LEVEL: Easy

FINISHED MEASUREMENTS:
11" x 9" x 1½" after felting

MATERIALS

4 skeins of Bullfrogs & Butterflies by Lorna's Laces (85% wool, 15% mohair; 113 g; 190 yds) in color 712 Farewell

Size 11 (8 mm) 20" circular needle or size required to obtain gauge

Stitch marker

Tapestry needle

2 rectangular metal rings, 1½"

2 lobster-claw clasps with attached metal ring, 1¼"

Becky's Glass breast-cancer button, 1" (optional; see "Resources" on page 79)

12" heavy-duty zipper

Sewing thread, needle, and pins

GAUGE

8 sts and 12 rows = 4" in St st before felting

NOTES

The purse is knit in one piece at a very loose gauge, and then felted in the washing machine. Use double strand of yarn throughout.

BASE

With double strand of yarn, CO 8 sts. Knit every row for 60 rows. BO.

PURSE SIDES

With double strand of yarn, *PU 30 sts along long edge, PU 8 sts along short edge; rep from * once—76 sts. Pm for beg of rnd.

Rnd 1: *K1, P1; rep from * around.

Rnd 2: *P1, K1; rep from * around.

Rep these 2 rnds until sides measure 14" from base. BO.

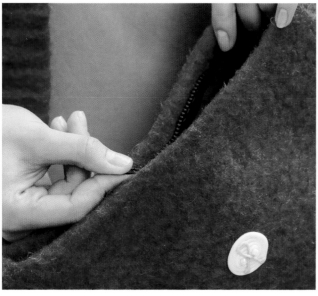
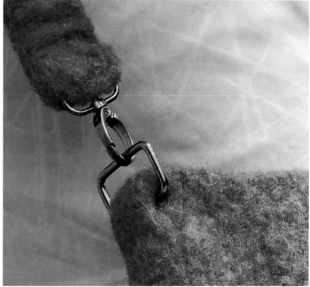

RING PATCHES

Make 2.

CO 4 sts. Work in St st for 4 rows. BO. Sew 1 patch to each short side of purse, even with top edge; insert metal ring under patch.

HANDLE

CO 7 sts. Work in garter st (knit every row) until handle measures 50". BO. Fold each end through the ring end of the lobster-claw closure and sew securely in place.

FINISHING

Weave in ends.

Place purse and handle in washing machine with jeans or other nonlinting item to add abrasion. Run on hot, regular-length cycle with laundry soap. Check frequently to determine how much felting has occurred. When bag has felted to desired size, remove from machine; make sure to do this before spin cycle. Rinse by hand in sink. Stretch and shape as needed. Bag can be manipulated and molded over a box or container to dry

(see "Felting" on page 77). Once dry, use electric razor or single-blade disposable razors to shave off excess fuzz. Shave in different directions. Pin zipper to inside edge, about ½" from top edge. Sew in place (see "Zippers" on page 76). Sew button to front (optional).

To wear, clip both ends of handle to one side of purse, with strap threaded through rectangular ring. Pull up just one strap to wear purse long, across body, like a messenger bag. Pull up both straps for a shorter shoulder bag.

Big Carryall Tote

The lining of this tote bag is its most important feature. It's fused in place, no sewing needed. The fusing method stabilizes the knitting, making a practical bag that doesn't stretch out of shape or sag. The suede bottom and handles are more than beautiful—they also add strength to the bag.

SKILL LEVEL: Beginner

FINISHED MEASUREMENTS:

12" x 13" x 4½"

MATERIALS

Cotton Fleece by Brown Sheep Company, Inc. (80% cotton, 20% wool; 100 g; 215 yds)

MC: 1 skein in color CW-900 Perry's Primrose

A: 1 skein in color CW-100 Cotton Ball

B: 1 skein in color CW-210 Tea Rose

C: 1 skein in color CW-220 Provincial Rose

Size 5 (3.75 mm) 16" circular and double-pointed needles or size required to obtain gauge

Tapestry needle

14" x 36" piece of cotton fabric for lining

14" x 36" piece of paper-backed fusible web

Iron

Sewing thread, needles, and pins

Large suede tote bottom (available from Somerset Designs; see "Resources" on page 79)

Pair of suede purse handles, 24" (available from Somerset Designs)

GAUGE

20 sts and 28 rows = 4" in stripe patt

STRIPE PATTERN

(Multiple of 8 sts)

Rows in *CC* are worked alternately in A, B, and C, changing color after each 12-row repeat.

Rows 1 and 2: With MC, knit.

Row 3 (RS): Change to *CC*, knit.

Rows 4–6: With *CC*, *K4, P4; rep from * across.

Rows 7 and 8: Change to MC, knit.

Row 9: Change to *CC*, knit.

Rows 10–12: With *CC*, *P4, K4; rep from * across.

Rep rows 1–12, working 1 complete rep with A, and then working next rep with B, followed by a third rep with C. Continue in this fashion, working each complete rep with each contrasting color in sequence.

TOTE BODY

The tote is knit sideways, back and forth. Cut yarn with each stripe, except for MC, tying knots at 1 edge. Trim yarn ends to 2"; do not weave in ends. Tuck ends between lining and fusible web and use this edge as the bottom edge of the tote; this bottom edge will be tucked inside the suede base.

With MC, CO 64 sts. Beg stripe patt. Work even for 33", ending after row 6 or 12. BO.

FINISHING

Block tote body very carefully, making sure it's straight and measures 33" long, exactly the circumference of the suede base. Cut lining fabric 1" longer and 1" wider. Fold 1 long edge down 1", making lining the same height as the knit tote. Fuse adhesive to the wrong side of fabric. Allow to cool. Peel off paper. Turn over and fuse to wrong side of knit tote, leaving 1" of length hanging over (be careful not to fuse this to the ironing board). Allow to cool. Sew CO edge to BO edge. Fuse extra 1" flap over seam. Insert tote into suede tote bottom. Pin in place. Sew through holes using running stitch or backstitch (see "Sewing Suede Bottoms" on page 77). Pin handles in place. Sew handles in place.

Stripe

8-st repeat

Key

- ▨ With MC, K on RS, P on WS
- ▣ With MC, P on RS, K on WS
- ☐ With CC, K on RS, P on WS
- ⊡ With CC, P on RS, K on WS

> ⫸ *Every test in our life makes us bitter or better; every problem comes to break us or make us. The choice is ours whether we become victim or victor.*
>
> ~Unknown

Soft Embrace Shawlette

The satiny, silky, drapey loveliness of this little shawl will be hard to resist. The knitting is fun also, with shaping and lace edgings happening at the same time.

SKILL LEVEL: Intermediate

FINISHED MEASUREMENTS: 56" x 16" at deepest point

MATERIALS

4 skeins of Romanza by Yarns of Italy (100% bamboo; 50 g; 112 yds) in color 172

Size 4 (3.5 mm) needles or size required to obtain gauge

Stitch markers

Tapestry needle

GAUGE

20 sts and 32 rows = 4" in St st

RIGHT BORDER

The right border, worked over first 5 sts, is the straight top edge as worn.

Row 1 and all odd-numbered rows (RS): Wyif, sl 1, K4.

Row 2 and all even-numbered rows: K5.

CENTER SECTION

Beg with 10 sts.

Row 1 and all odd-numbered rows (RS): Knit.

Rows 2, 4, 6, 8, 10, and 12: Purl.

Row 14 (WS): Knit.

LEFT BORDER

The left border is the decorative, curved lower edge as worn.

Beg with 13 sts.

Rows 1 (RS): K4, YO, K5, YO, K2tog, YO, K2—15 sts.

Rows 2, 4, 6, 8, 10, and 12: Purl.

Row 3: K5, sl 1, K2tog, psso, K2, (YO, K2tog) twice, K1—13 sts.

Row 5: K4, ssk, K2, (YO, K2tog) twice, K1—11 sts.

Row 7: K3, ssk, K2, (YO, K2tog) twice, K1—11 sts.

Row 9: K2, ssk, K2, (YO, K2tog) twice, K1—10 sts.

Row 11: K1, ssk, K2, YO, K1, YO, K2tog, YO, K2—11 sts.

Row 13: K1, (K3, YO) twice, K2tog, YO, K2—13 sts.

Row 14 (WS): Knit.

SHAWL

CO 28 sts. Work 5 sts right border, pm, work 10 sts center section, pm, work 13 sts left border. Work even in patt until work measures 10", ending after a WS row.

INCREASES

Work across right border, knit across center section to last st, work lifted inc (page 75), K1, continue in patt across left border.

Continue in patt, inc 1 st at end of center section every RS row until there are 60 sts in center section. Work even in patt for 10".

DECREASES

Work across right border, knit across center section to last 2 sts, K2tog, continue in patt across left border. Work dec every RS row until there are 10 sts in center section. Work even in patt for 10".

BO.

FINISHING

Weave in ends. Block.

> ⋙ *On May 5, 2003, I was diagnosed with breast cancer. Through the recovery of losing both breasts, I was taught how to crochet by a friend and how to knit by my sister. I don't know what I would have done without these two arts to help me through a tough and lonely journey. I found myself needing to be around yarn, texture, and color. Out of my love for fiber art grew a desire to open a shop. If knitting and crochet could give me such joy during a sad and lonely journey, then maybe others could benefit and love it too!*
>
> *~Anna, owner of Anna's Yarn Shoppe, Elk Grove, CA*

Wavy left border

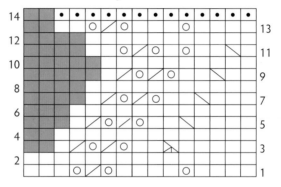

13-st border

Key

⊡	YO
⊠	Sl 1, K2tog, psso
╱	Ssk
╲	K2tog
☐	K on RS, P on WS
⊡	K on WS
▨	No stitch

Summer's Embrace Shawlette

Sometimes less is more. This shawl uses just a touch of variegated color-changing yarn, making it a subtle highlight to be treasured. The unusual shape of this long shawlette allows it to be worn many different ways.

SKILL LEVEL: Intermediate

FINISHED MEASUREMENTS:
45" x 45"

MATERIALS

Fingering by Freia Fine Handpaint Yarns (75% wool, 25% nylon; 50 g; 215 yds)

MC: 3 skeins in color Garnet

CC: 1 skein in color Flare Ombré

Size 8 (5 mm) needles or size required to obtain gauge

Open stitch markers (variety)

Tapestry needle

GAUGE

19 sts and 40 rows = 4" in garter st after blocking

FEATHER AND FAN PATTERN

(Multiple of 11 sts)

Row 1 (RS): Knit.

Row 2: Purl.

Row 3: *K2tog twice, (YO, K1) 3 times, YO, K2tog twice; rep from * across.

Row 4: Knit.

Rep rows 1–4 for patt.

SHAWL

Shawl begins at the neck edge. Incs are worked every RS row in 4 places.

With MC, CO 145 sts.

Next row (WS): *P1, pm through center of corner st, K47; rep from * across, P1.

Next row: *K1, YO, knit to marked st, YO; rep from * across, K1.

Next row: *P1, knit to marked st; rep from * across, P1.

Rep these 2 rows 8 more times (18 rows total). Do not cut yarn.

Join CC and work 2 rows in patt as established. Cut CC. Continue to alternate 18 rows MC and 2 rows CC until there are 143 sts on each side between marked sts.

With CC, beg feather and fan patt. Place additional markers at beg and end of feather and fan patt on each side. Work new sts in St st until another 11 sts have been increased (enough for another patt rep). Continue in patt until border measures 2". BO using picot method (See "Picot Bind Off" on page 76).

FINISHING

Weave in ends.

Feather and fan

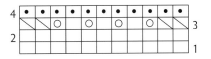

11-st repeat

Key

⬜ K2tog

⬜ YO

⬛ K on RS, P on WS

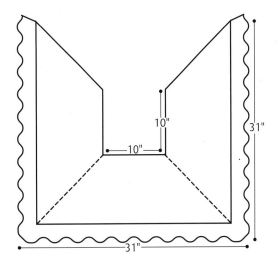

Cuddly Reversible Stole

This is specifically an openwork shawl, not lace—the knitting is too simple to call it lace. The pattern is completely reversible and identical on both sides. It will knit up quickly and enjoyably!

SKILL LEVEL: Easy

FINISHED MEASUREMENTS:

20" x 56"

MATERIALS

6 skeins of Classic Chunky by Universal Yarn (75% acrylic, 25% wool; 100 g; 131 yds) in color 60614 Light Pink

Size 11 (8 mm) needles or size required to obtain gauge

Row counter

Tapestry needle

GAUGE

10 sts and 18 rows = 4" in reversible openwork patt

NOTES

It's advisable to use row counter to keep track of rows since both sides look the same. Do not count sts after rows 1 or 8. Number of sts will return to original number after rows 3 and 10.

REVERSIBLE OPENWORK PATTERN

(Multiple of 2 sts)

Row 1: K1, *YO, K1; rep from * to last st, K1.

Row 2: K1, purl to last st, K1.

Row 3: K1, *K2tog; rep from * to last st, K1.

Rows 4 and 5: K1, *YO, K2tog; rep from * to last st, K1.

Rows 6 and 7: Knit.

Row 8: K1, *YO, K1; rep from * to last st, K1.

Row 9: K1, purl to last st, K1.

Row 10: K1, *K2tog; rep from * to last st, K1.

Rows 11 and 12: K1, *YO, K2tog; rep from * to last st, K1.

Rows 13 and 14: Knit.

Rep rows 1–14 for patt.

STOLE

CO 50 sts. Work in reversible openwork patt until stole measures 56". BO very loosely.

FINISHING

Weave in ends. Block.

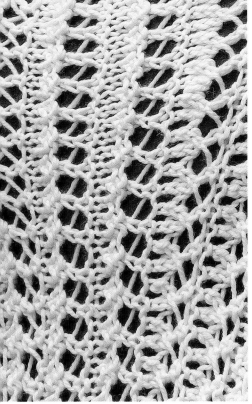

Hugs and Squeezes Shrug

This shrug is not only beautiful, but it's also handy. It slips over one's arms without falling off or needing a shawl pin. It will cover light clothing without the bulk of a sweater. And the lace will brighten anyone's day!

SKILL LEVEL: Intermediate

FINISHED MEASUREMENTS:
48" (cuff to cuff) x 19" long, unstretched

MATERIALS

MC: 1 skein of Haiku by Anzula Luxury Fibers (70% superwash merino, 20% bamboo, 10% nylon; 114 g; 500 yds) in color Black Cherry

CC: 1 skein of Oasis by Anzula Luxury Fibers (70% camel, 30% silk; 114 g; 375 yds) in color Boysenberry

Size 8 (5 mm) straight and double-pointed needles or size required to obtain gauge

Tapestry needle

GAUGE

22 sts and 24 rows = 4" in 2 x 2 ribbing patt, unstretched

2 x 2 RIBBING PATTERN

(Multiple of 4 + 2 sts)

Row 1 (RS): *K2, P2; rep from * to last 2 sts, K2.

Row 2: *P2, K2; rep from * to last 2 sts, P2.

Rep rows 1 and 2 for patt.

CHEVRON LACE PATTERN

(Multiple of 10 sts)

Rnd 1: *YO, K3, sl 1, K2tog, psso, K3, YO, K1; rep from * around.

Rnd 2: Knit.

Rnd 3: *K1, YO, K2, sl 1, K2tog, psso, K2, YO, K2; rep from * around.

Rnd 4: Knit.

Rep rnds 1–4 for patt.

SHRUG BODY

Body of shrug is worked first; then lace cuffs are picked up and worked around the bottom of each sleeve.

With MC, CO 106 sts, work in
2 x 2 ribbing patt for 4 rows.
Do not cut yarn. Join CC and
cont in patt for 4 rows. Carry
unused yarn loosely up side of
work. Cont in 2 x 2 ribbing patt,
changing colors every 4 rows
until piece measures 36". Cut
CC. BO.

Fold in half lengthwise. Sew side
edges tog 7" in from each end to
make sleeves.

LACE CUFFS

With double-pointed needles
and MC, PU 100 sts along
CO edge. Pm for beg of rnd.
Work in chevron lace patt for 6".
BO loosely. Rep lace edging on
BO edge.

FINISHING

Weave in ends. Block.

> ⋙ *If you stumble, make
> it part of the dance!*
>
> ~*Unknown*

Chevron lace

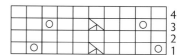

11-st repeat
Work all rnds from right to left.

Key

⊠ Sl 1, K2tog, psso

◻ YO

☐ K

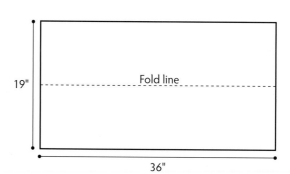

Comfy Socks

The stitch pattern of these socks is designed to blend hand-dyed yarns and create a mix of color with less pooling or unintentional patterning. Also, the color Flamingo Stripe is very special; Lorna's Laces created this color specifically to donate 20% of the proceeds to breast-cancer charities. What a great combination!

SKILL LEVEL: Intermediate

SIZES: To fit women's US shoes sizes 5 to 6½ (women's sizes 8½ to 10)

FINISHED MEASUREMENTS: Approx 7¼ (8½)" circumference x 8½ (10)" long from back of heel to tip of toe

MATERIALS

1 skein of Shepherd Sock by Lorna's Laces (75% wool, 25% nylon; 100 g; 430 yds) in color 507 Flamingo Stripe

Size 1 (2.25 mm) double-pointed needles or size required to obtain gauge

Stitch marker

Tapestry needle

GAUGE

28 sts and 34 rnds = 4" in alternating rib patt

ALTERNATING RIB PATTERN

(Multiple of 2 sts)

Rnds 1–4: *K1, P1; rep from * around.

Rnds 5–8: *P1, P1; rep from * around.

Rep rnds 1–8 for patt.

LEG

Loosely CO 52 (60) sts. Divide sts as evenly as possible on 3 double-pointed needles. Pm and join, being careful not to twist the sts. Rnd begins at back of leg. Work in alternating rib patt until piece measures about 7 (8)" from CO, or desired length to heel, ending after row 4 or 8.

HEEL FLAP

Heel is worked back and forth in rows on 26 (30) sts.

Row 1 (RS): *Sl 1, K1; rep from * across.

Row 2: Sl 1, purl.

Rep rows 1 and 2 until 26 (30) heel-flap rows have been completed, ending after row 2.

HEEL TURN

Turn heel as follows:

Row 1 (RS): Sl 1, K14 (16), ssk, K1, turn.

Row 2: Sl 1, P5, P2tog, P1, turn.

Row 3: Sl 1, K6, ssk, K1, turn.

Row 4: Sl 1, P7, P2tog, P1, turn.

Rep rows 3 and 4, inc 1 additional knit or purl st after the sl 1 until all side sts have been worked, ending after WS row.

SHAPE GUSSETS

Knit to center of heel. With spare needle, knit across rem heel sts. With first needle, PU 13 (15) sts from side of heel flap and K1 st in gusset corner—22 (25) sts. With second needle, work in patt across—26 (30) sts. With third needle, PU 1 st in gusset corner, and then PU 13 (15) sts from side of heel flap. Knit rem heel sts—22 (25) sts. Rnds now begin at center of heel.

Rnd 2: On first needle, knit to last 3 sts, K2tog, K1; on second needle, work in patt as established; on third needle, K1, ssk, knit to end—2 sts dec.

Rnd 3: Cont in patt as established (work sts on second needle in patt; work sts on first and third needles in St st).

Work rnds 2 and 3 another 8 (9) times—52 (60) sts.

FOOT

Work even in patt until foot measures about 6¾ (8)" from back of heel, or about 1¾ (2)" less than desired total foot length, ending after rnd 4 or 8.

SHAPE TOE

Rnd 1: On first needle, knit to last 2 sts, K2tog; on second needle, ssk, knit to last 3 sts, K2tog; on third needle, ssk, knit to end—4 sts dec.

Rnd 2: Knit.

Work rnds 1 and 2 another 7 (8) times—20 (24) sts rem.

FINISHING

Cut yarn, leaving 12" tail. Thread tail on yarn needle and use Kitchener st (page 75) to graft sts tog. Weave in ends. Block lightly.

Alternating rib

2-st repeat
Work all rnds from right to left.

Key

□• P
□ K

Biased Love
Vest or Jacket

Make this with or without sleeves. It's easy to throw on over anything and looks so stylish. The flowing, easy-fitting style makes it practical for anyone to wear.

SKILL LEVEL: Easy

SIZES: Small/Medium (Large/XL, 2X/3X)

FINISHED MEASUREMENTS:

To fit bust: 32–36 (38–44, 46–56)"

Back length: 18 (22, 28)"

Sleeve length: 18 (19, 20)"

MATERIALS

Sleeveless version: 3 (4, 5) skeins of Haven by Shalimar Yarns (63% merino, 37% tussah silk; 100 g; 247 yds) in color Petal

Sleeved version: 7 (9, 12) skeins of Loden by Grignasco Knits (50% virgin wool, 25% alpaca, 25% viscose; 50 g; 120 yds) in color 637

Size 8 (5 mm) needles or size required to obtain gauge

Tapestry needle

GAUGE

16 sts and 22 rows = 4" in St st

NOTES

The back is knit first from the bottom up. Each front is then picked up and knit downward from the shoulder. Because the front is knit on the bias, the front is knit until it's the same length as the back, rather than according to a specific number of stitches. The front panels drape at an angle and can be worn loose and open or overlapped at the waist with a shawl pin.

BACK

CO 88 (104, 128) sts. Working in St st, dec 1 st at each edge every 8th row 8 times—72 (88, 112) sts. Work even until back measures 14 (16, 18)". Pm on each edge for armhole opening. Work even until armhole measures 8 (9, 10)", ending after a WS row.

SHAPE SHOULDERS

Slipping first st of each BO, BO 3 (4, 6) sts at beg of every row 12 times. BO 4 (4, 2) sts at beg of last 2 rows. BO rem 28 (32, 36) sts for neck edge.

RIGHT FRONT

With RS facing you, PU 22 (28, 38) sts from right-back shoulder BO. Working in St st, Kfb at beg of every RS row until right edge measures same as side edge of back. BO all sts. BO edge is front hem, which swings upward; left edge is V-neck part of center front.

LEFT FRONT

With RS facing you, PU 22 (28, 38) sts from left-back shoulder BO. Working in St st, Kfb at end of every RS row. Continue inc until left edge measures same as side edge of back. BO all sts. BO edge is front hem, which swings upward; right edge is V-neck part of center front.

SLEEVES

Optional; make 2.

Measure 8 (9, 10)" down from shoulder on front and back side edges, pm.

With RS facing you, PU 56 (64, 72) sts between markers. Working in St st, dec 1 st at each edge every 8th (6th, 6th) row 12 (14, 16) times—32 (36, 40) sts. Work even until sleeve measures 20 (19, 18)" or desired length to cuff. BO.

FINISHING

For sleeveless version, sew side seams, leaving armhole open (see "Mattress Seam" on page 76).

For sleeved version, sew side seams and underarm seams (see "Mattress Seam.")

Weave in ends. Block.

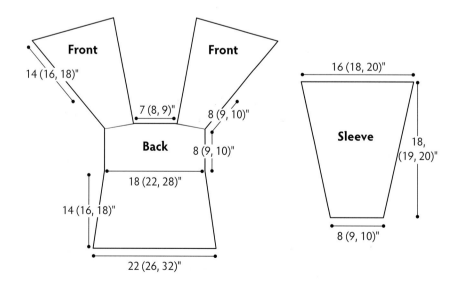

Snuggly Slippers

Slippers, socks, mukluks—whatever you call them, they are cozy warm, last forever, and the suede soles are available in a variety of colors.

SKILL LEVEL: Easy

SIZES: 11 sizes, from babies to adults

FINISHED MEASUREMENTS:

Child: 4 (5, 6, 7, 8)" long

Adult: 9 (9½, 10, 10½, 11, 12)" long

MATERIALS

Lamb's Pride Worsted by Brown Sheep Company, Inc. (85% wool, 15% mohair; 113 g; 190 yds)

MC: 1 skein in color M-105 RPM Pink

CC: 1 skein in color M-05 Onyx

Size 7 (4.5 mm) double-pointed needles or size required to obtain gauge

Tapestry needle

1 pair of black suede slipper soles in desired size (available from Somerset Designs; see "Resources" on page 79)

Sewing needle and embroidery floss or sock yarn

GAUGE

18 sts and 20 rows = 4" in stripe patt

STRIPE PATTERN

Row 1 (RS): With MC, knit.

Row 2: With MC, purl.

Row 3: With MC, knit.

Row 4: With MC, purl.

Row 5: With CC, knit.

Row 6: With CC, knit.

SLIPPERS

The leg portion is knit flat, side to side. After joining the CO and BO edges to form a tube, stitches are then picked up along bottom edge and worked downward for the foot portion. There is no knit sole—the suede sole is used instead.

Leg

Throughout patt, first group of numbers is the child sizes; second group is adult.

With MC, CO 14 (14, 18, 18, 18) 22 (22, 22, 22, 28, 28) sts. Work in stripe patt until leg measures 6 (6, 6, 6, 7) 8 (8, 9, 9, 10, 10)".

BO all sts. Sew CO edge to BO edge.

Foot

With MC, PU 24 (24, 28, 28, 32) 36 (36, 40, 40, 44, 44) sts around bottom edge of leg. Divide sts over 3 dpns. Pm for beg of rnd. Knit 2 rnds.

Heel

Knit across first 12 (12, 14, 14, 16) 18 (18, 20, 20, 22, 22) sts. Turn and purl back. Work back and forth in stripe patt on these sts only for 8 (8, 10, 10, 12) 12 (12, 14, 14, 14, 14) rows. BO heel sts on next RS row but do not break yarn.

Instep and Gussets

PU 4 (4, 5, 5, 6) 6 (6, 7, 7, 7, 7) sts along side of heel, pm, knit across 12 (12, 14, 14, 16) 18 (18, 20, 20, 22, 22) sts across top of foot, pm, PU 4 (4, 5, 5, 6) 6 (6, 7, 7, 7, 7) sts along side of heel. Turn and purl across.

Next row (RS): Knit to 2 sts before marker, K2tog, sl marker, knit to next marker, sl marker, ssk, knit to end.

Next row: Purl.

Rep from * until only 1 st rem outside of markers. Remove markers and work even in St st until length of foot from back of heel to toe measures 3 (4, 4, 5, 6) 7 (7, 7, 7½, 8, 9)".

BO 4 sts at beg of next 2 rows. BO rem sts.

Finishing

Weave in ends. Pin slipper top to inside of suede soles, centering at heel and toe first, and then along sides. With embroidery floss or sock yarn, sew sole to slipper using backstitch (see "Sewing Suede Bottoms" on page 77).

>≫ *I think by not focusing too hard it's easier to stay encouraged. Live in the moment. Know what to be angry at: if you're wiping a dog's muddy footprints off your kitchen floor for the tenth time that day, that will piss you off as much as cancer, only the footprints you* can *clean up.*
>
> *~Ann, www.ButDoctorIHatePink.com*

Beauty Facecloths

Little facecloths and washcloths make wonderful gifts. They're quick, too. Here are two different ways to show your love with hearts!

SKILL LEVEL: Easy

FINISHED MEASUREMENTS:
Approx 8" x 8"

MATERIALS

2 skeins of Lunare by Yarns of Italy (100% cotton; 50 g; 85 yds) in color 1304 *

Size 6 (4 mm) needles or size required to obtain gauge

Tapestry needle

Yarn is enough for both facecloths

GAUGE

18 sts and 24 rows = 4" in garter st

Mitered Heart Facecloth

CO 25 sts, pm, CO 25 sts—50 sts.

Row 1 (RS): Kfb, knit to 2 sts before marker, K2tog, sl marker, K2tog, knit to end, Kfb.

Row 2: Knit.

Rows 3–14: Rep rows 1 and 2.

Row 15: Knit to 2 sts before marker, K2tog, sl marker, K2tog, knit to end—2 sts dec.

Row 16: Knit.

Rows 17–26: Rep rows 15 and 16—38 sts.

Row 27: K2tog, knit to 2 sts before marker, K2tog, sl marker, K2tog, knit to last 2 sts, K2tog—4 sts dec.

Row 28: Knit.

Rows 29–34: Rep rows 27 and 28—22 sts.

BO.

FINISHING

Weave in ends. Block.

Textured Heart Facecloth

CO 35 sts. Follow chart on page 72 from right to left for right-side rows and from left to right for wrong-side rows. When 48 rows of chart are complete, BO.

FINISHING

Weave in ends. Block.

Textured heart

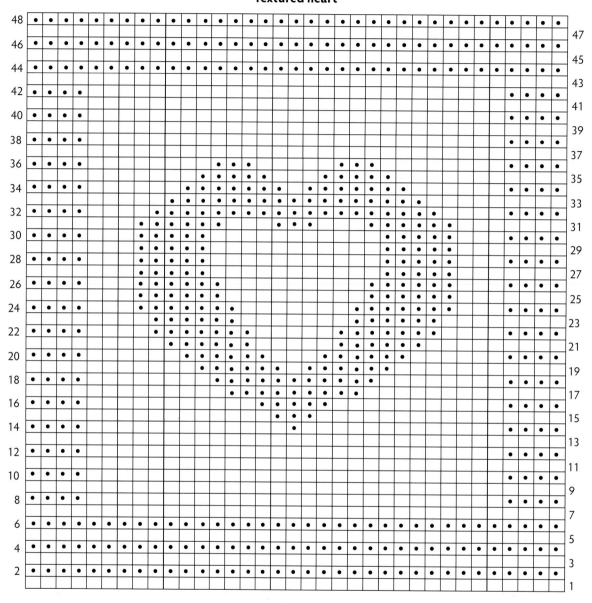

Key

• P on RS, K on WS

☐ K on RS, P on WS

Knitting Techniques

In this section, you'll find an introduction to the various techniques used in the construction of these projects. Once you know how to knit, purl, cast on, and bind off, everything else is a variation on these. Reading the abbreviations and special instructions carefully will help you to re-create what the designer has done.

CHOOSING YARNS

All of the projects here are made with soft, high-quality yarns. Be sure to choose fibers that will comfort sensitive skin, especially when knitting chemo hats and scarves. For lap throws, choose real wool for warmth—ideally something washable so the throw can be used and enjoyed without inhibition.

Yarn labels identify the fiber content of the yarn. Try to choose a yarn similar in fiber content to the original pattern. Also refer to the yardage and recommended stitch gauge on the label and compare that to the pattern for similarity in weight and to determine how much yarn you'll need. Always use yardage, rather than ounces or grams, for determining how much yarn to buy.

If a pattern calls for bamboo or silk, don't replace the yarn with acrylic or wool. Yarn choice is much more than just getting the same gauge; it affects the drape of the item, how the stitch pattern shows up, and how a garment fits. Some fibers are slippery with no memory or bounce to them; these fibers include bamboo, silk, alpaca, and cotton. Other fibers, such as wool and acrylic blends, tend to keep their shape and are more resilient.

Some of the luxury yarns can be costly. When you consider your time investment (not to mention pleasure!) in knitting the project, plus the years of appreciation that it will bring, the cost is easily justifiable. You and the recipient *will* be able to tell the difference!

TOOLS

One of the beautiful things about knitting is how portable it is. With just yarn and needles, you can hit the road, plane, bus, coffee shop, or waiting room. But there are a few little items that can make knitting easier. You should consider carrying the following with you in a small pencil case or zippered bag:

- Tape measure, for measuring gauge and knitting in progress
- Small scissors
- Tapestry needle, for weaving in ends
- Needle sizer, in case the numbers on the needle are hard to read
- A few stitch markers, including some that open
- Emery board, for smooth fingernails
- A few small binder clips from the office-supply store, for "pinning" seams together without snagging

DOUBLE-POINTED NEEDLES

When working a hat decrease or other small number of stitches in the round, it will become necessary to use double-pointed needles. Double-pointed needles come in sets of four or five, in lengths as short as 4", though most are about 8" long. They're used primarily for knitting in the round over circumferences that are too small for a circular needle, but they can also be used in pairs to knit I-cord. When casting on with double-pointed needles, cast all of the stitches on a single needle first, and then arrange the stitches as evenly as possible over three (or four) needles. With the final needle, knit the stitches on the first needle, then use this (now) empty needle to knit the stitches on the second needle, and so forth.

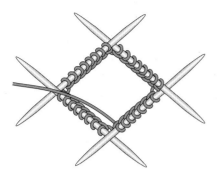

DECREASES

K2tog (knit two stitches together). The simple K2tog decrease leans to the right, with the left stitch lying on top of the right one. It decreases the stitch count by one stitch.

Insert the right needle through the second and first stitches on the left needle together and work them as one stitch.

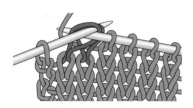

Ssk (slip, slip, knit two stitches together). This decrease leans to the left, with the right stitch lying on top of the left one. It decreases the stitch count by one stitch.

Slip each of these stitches as if to knit; then insert the left-needle tip into both stitches together from the left.

DOUBLE DECREASES

S2KP (slip two stitches together knitwise, knit one stitch, pass two slipped stitches over). This double decrease keeps the center stitch on top.

Slip the first two stitches together as if you were going to knit them together. Knit the next stitch, and then pass the two slipped stitches over the stitch that was knit.

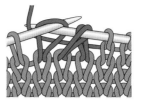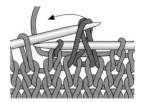

Sl 1, K2tog, psso (slip one stitch as if to knit, knit two stitches together, pass the slipped stitch over). This double decrease keeps the right stitch on top.

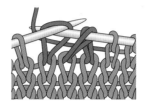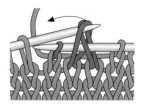

INCREASES

Kfb (knit into the front and back of the stitch). Knit into the stitch the normal way, but do not remove it from the left needle. Now knit into the back of the stitch. One stitch is increased.

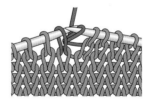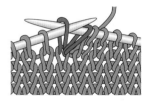

YO (yarn over). This increase makes a decorative hole. Wrap the yarn over the right needle, the same way you would if the needle was in a stitch, from the front to the back.

M1 (make one). Insert the right needle under the bar of yarn between the last stitch on the right needle and the first stitch on the left needle. Lift the bar onto the left needle and knit it through the back loop. One stitch is increased.

Lifted inc (lifted increase). Insert right needle in purl bump on wrong side of row below; place on left needle and knit through this stitch. One stitch is increased.

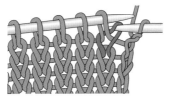

OTHER STITCH

K1b (knit into the row below). Carefully insert the needle into the center of the stitch one row below the needle, all the way through to the back; wrap the yarn around and pull it through as for a normal knit stitch.

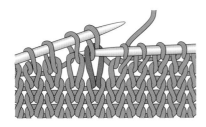

I-CORD

I-cord is a way to make a knitted cord using just three or four stitches. You need to use double-pointed needles (page 73).

Using double-pointed needles, cast on three or four stitches. *Do not turn work. Slide stitches to right end of needle and knit across; repeat from * until I-cord measures the desired length.

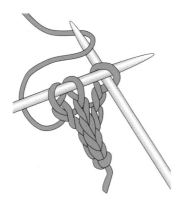

KITCHENER STITCH

The Kitchener stitch is a method for grafting live stitches together at the top so that the join looks like another row of knitting. It's commonly used to sew closed the toe of a sock. Pull the yarn all the way through the stitch after each step, but not too tightly, and keep the yarn below the needles.

1. Place the stitches on two needles, with the same number on each needle. Hold the two needles so the garment wrong sides are together.
2. Cut the yarn at least three times longer than the width of stitches. Thread a tapestry needle. Insert the needle in the first stitch on the front needle as if to purl. Do not take the stitch off the needle yet.
3. Insert the tapestry needle through the first stitch on the back needle as if to knit; do not remove that stitch from the needle yet.
4. Insert the tapestry needle through the same (first) stitch on the front needle, this time as if to knit. Now remove this stitch from the needle.
5. Insert the tapestry needle through the next stitch on the front needle as if to purl; do not remove the stitch.
6. Insert the tapestry needle through the same (first) stitch on the back needle as if to purl; remove this stitch from the needle.
7. Insert the tapestry needle through the next stitch on the back needle as if to knit; do not remove the stitch.
8. Repeat steps 4–7 until all stitches have been used. To keep the correct order, it may help to remember this mantra: "knit, purl front; purl, knit back."

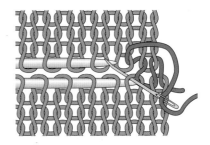

PICOT BIND OFF

A *picot* is a small clump or bump of stitches on an edge for decoration. The stitches take time, but are a pretty, feminine touch.

Knit version. *Cast on four stitches to the left-needle tip; bind off these same four stitches plus the next four stitches on the needle; rep from * across, ending with a picot (cast on four, bind off four).

Quicker crochet version. With a crochet hook, insert the hook into the first stitch, *chain four, slip stitch in same stitch, bind off four stitches; repeat from * across.

The crochet version is slightly less bulky and works faster, but a little crochet skill is needed.

JOINING YARN AND HIDING ENDS

It's usually best to start a new ball of yarn along an edge, especially if that edge will be used for a seam. If the project doesn't have seams, look for a place in the pattern that has a change of texture or stitch pattern. This can help disguise the extra layer of yarn. Weave each yarn end in opposite directions. I usually follow along a row or column of stitches on the wrong side.

MATTRESS SEAM

For vertical seams such as side seams, try this invisible seam method. It will be easy to see how it looks because you work it from the right side. I like to hold the seam together using binder clips from an office-supply store. This keeps my seams lined up even if the rows vary (as they do in the Biased Love Vest or Jacket on page 65). Clip the edges together at the top and bottom and every 3–4" in between. I prefer to leave long yarn tails from my cast on to use for seaming.

Thread a tapestry needle with the seaming yarn. Insert the needle down through the center of the edge stitch on the left side, and then up through the center of the next row up (or skip one row). Pull the yarn snug but not tight. Repeat for the right side. Working alternately up the edge, the clips will

help you keep the seaming even. Usually this is done evenly, matching each side row for row.

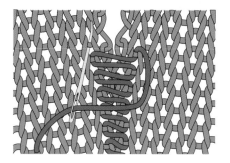

ZIPPERS

Sewing zippers into knitting is often tricky because the knitting stretches and moves. However, for the two projects in this book that have zippers, this is not the case. One project (Handy Little Clutch, page 41) is lined, which stabilizes the knitting, and the other project (Classy Felted Purse, page 45) is felted. The important thing to keep in mind is to pin the zipper to both edges, making sure they line up. It's OK to have excess zipper at either or both ends. That can be hidden or trimmed later. Also, the zipper can be sewn to the very edge of the knitting, or moved a little bit away from the edge to hide it. I like to sew the zipper very close to the teeth using a backstitch. I also sew the edge of the tape down.

FUSED LINING

I use fused lining not just to eliminate a sewing machine, but because fusing stabilizes the knitting, which makes for a far more practical knit bag. All fusing is done either on the paper side of the adhesive or on the fabric side, never on the side of the knitting. The measurements are simpler than they seem. Rather than simply lining the exact measurements of the bag, I like to add a small allowance for overlapping. The result looks nicer and keeps small things like knitting needles or pencils from poking through the gap. The top edge has a small allowance added for folding down and making a smooth edge. I like to sew this edge invisibly to the inside of the bag for extra durability. Don't be too picky—this is the inside of a bag and will be hidden by the contents that get added!

FELTING

Felting is the process of shrinking the wool fibers to become a solid piece of fabric. In some cases, the knitting can be shrunk so thoroughly that the stitches are no longer visible. The choice is yours how much you felt a project. Hats, slippers, and mittens need to fit a body part, so they can't be felted too much. However, a purse or pillow can be felted as much or as little as you like.

Felting is best done in a washing machine; it takes a very long time to do it by hand. Use a regular wash cycle and hot water. Put the knitted item in the machine along with laundry detergent and an old pair of jeans. Don't use new jeans that might leach color or shrink, and don't use terry-cloth towels that will put lint and fuzz all over your felted item. The jeans add agitation—something for the knitting to rub against to help it felt faster and more evenly. Run the washer as usual, but at the end of the agitation cycle, remove the item and check the shrinkage. If you like it, remove it from the washer. If you want more shrinkage, turn the washer back to the beginning of the agitation cycle.

Allow the item to air dry. While it's wet, you can tug and mold it to the shape you like. If it's twisted or distorted, pull hard in the opposite direction to straighten. You can shape it over a box or bowl to give it a more precise shape.

Once dry, it's done! Or, if you like a more finished look, you can shave your felted item. Use a set of small electric clippers or the cheap, single-blade razors found at dollar stores. Just shave slowly over the whole project in one direction, and then shave again in several other directions for a sophisticated, smooth felted look.

BLOCKING

Blocking is what evens out and "crisps" the shape of a project, especially projects with rolling edges, lace, or shaped borders. You'll need blocking wires or a lot of rustproof pins, a thick blanket or foam blocking boards, a ruler, and a place with room to spread out the project (preferably animal-free!).

Fill a sink with warm water. Place the project in the sink and allow it to soak for 30 minutes. While it's soaking, spread out the blocking boards or blanket. Gently squeeze as much water out of the project as possible without twisting it. Spread it out on the blocking surface. Pull the edges straight, the points out, the corners pointed, etc. If using blocking wires, run them in and out of the outer edge, and then pin the long wire in just a few places. Blocking wires make blocking a scarf or shawl very easy! Once everything is pinned, allow it to dry. To help it along, point a fan at it (never heat), and it will likely be dry in a few hours.

If a yarn is 90%–100% wool or other natural animal fiber, it can be steamed rather than blocked wet. Just spread it out and pin it, and then hold a steam iron hovering ½" above the surface while pushing the steam button. Do not let the iron touch the project.

SEWING SUEDE BOTTOMS

The suede tote bottom and slipper soles from Somerset Designs (see "Resources" on page 79) come assembled with prepunched holes. This not only makes sewing them to your knitted items easy, but the stitches look even and professionally done with little skill needed! Before sewing, pin the knitting to the suede. Make sure the knitting is evenly spaced all around the suede and there are no gaps. The suede will not give, so the size of the knitting has to match perfectly. Once pinned, begin with a long piece of yarn or thread where the suede is seamed. Use the same method for sewing on the suede purse handles.

Thread a small, sharp darning needle, the smallest one that you can get your thread or yarn through. You can use a whipstitch, blanket stitch, or any decorative stitch you'd like. I usually use a running stitch or a backstitch as shown on page 78.

Running stitch. *Bring the needle up through both layers and through a hole in the suede. Insert the needle down through the next hole and through both layers. Repeat from * around. Keep the thread snug and even. Tie a knot at the end and weave in the yarn ends.

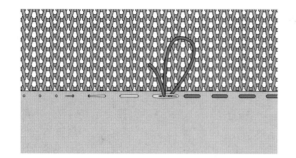

Backstitch. Bring the needle up through both layers and through the *second* hole in the suede. *Insert the needle down through the *first* hole (backward). Bring the needle up through both layers, skipping a hole, and through the next empty hole. Repeat from * around. When inserting the needle downward, it will be the second time the yarn passes through that hole.

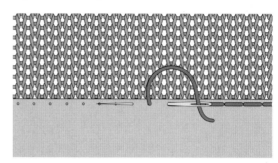

Knitting Abbreviations

() Work instructions within parentheses in the place directed.

* Repeat instructions following the single asterisk as directed.

approx approximately

beg begin(ning)

BO bind off

CC contrasting color

cn cable needle

CO cast on

cont continue

dec decrease(ing)

dpn double-pointed needles

g gram(s)

inc increase(ing)

K knit

K1b knit into the row below

K2tog knit 2 stitches together

Kfb knit into front and back of st

LH left hand

lp(s) loop(s)

M1 make 1 stitch

MC main color

oz ounce(s)

P purl

P2tog purl 2 stitches together

patt pattern

pm place marker

psso pass slipped stitch over

PU pick up and knit

pw purlwise

rem remaining

rep repeat

RH right hand

rnd(s) round(s)

RS right side(s)

S2KP slip 2 together knitwise, K1, pass 2 slipped sts over (centered double decrease made)

Sl slip

Sl 1, K2tog, psso slip 1 stitch as if to knit, knit 2 stitches together, pass slipped stitch over (double decrease made)

sl st slip stitch

ssk slip, slip, knit these 2 stitches together

st(s) stitch(es)

St st stockinette stitch

tbl through back loop

tog together

WS wrong side(s)

wyif with yarn in front

yd(s) yard(s)

YO yarn over

Helpful Information

YARN WEIGHTS							
Yarn-Weight Symbol and Category Name	**0** Lace	**1** Super Fine	**2** Fine	**3** Light	**4** Medium	**5** Bulky	**6** Super Bulky
Types of Yarn in Category	Fingering, 10-count crochet thread	Sock, Fingering, Baby	Sport, Baby	DK, Light Worsted	Worsted, Afghan, Aran	Chunky, Craft, Rug	Bulky, Roving
Knit Gauge Range in Stockinette Stitch to 4"*	33 to 40 sts	27 to 32 sts	23 to 26 sts	21 to 24 sts	16 to 20 sts	12 to 15 sts	6 to 11 sts
Recommended Needle in Metric Size Range	1.5 to 2.25 mm	2.25 to 3.25 mm	3.25 to 3.75 mm	3.75 to 4.5 mm	4.5 to 5.5 mm	5.5 to 8 mm	8 mm and larger
Recommended Needle in US Size Range	000 to 1	1 to 3	3 to 5	5 to 7	7 to 9	9 to 11	11 and larger

The above guidelines reflect the most commonly used gauges and needle or hook sizes for specific yarn categories. Lace-weight yarns are often knitted on larger needles to create lacy, openwork patterns. Accordingly, a gauge range is difficult to determine. Always follow the gauge stated in your pattern.

METRIC CONVERSIONS

Yards x .91 = meters
Meters x 1.09 = yards
Grams x .035 = ounces
Ounces x 28.35 = grams

RESOURCES

Contact the following companies to find shops that carry the yarns and notions featured in this book.

Alchemy Yarns of Transformation
www.alchemyyarns.com
Migrations

Anzula Luxury Fibers
www.anzula.com
Haiku, Oasis

Becky's Glass
www.beckysglass.etsy.com
Glass breast-cancer button (available by special request)

Berroco, Inc.
www.berroco.com
Comfort DK

Brown Sheep Company, Inc.
www.brownsheep.com
Cotton Fleece, Lamb's Pride Worsted, Nature Spun Chunky

Classic Elite Yarns
www.classiceliteyarns.com
Fresco

Freia Fine Handpaint Yarns
www.freiafibers.com
Fingering, Sport, Worsted

Kollage Yarns
www.kollageyarns.com
Scrumptious

Kraemer Yarns
www.kraemeryarns.com
Tatamy

Lorna's Laces
www.lornaslaces.net
Bullfrogs & Butterflies, Shepherd Sock, Shepherd Worsted

Plymouth Yarn Company Inc.
www.plymouthyarn.com
Angora Glitz, Encore Tweed, Encore Worsted, Loden by Grignasco Knits, Worsted Merino Superwash

Shalimar Yarns
www.shalimaryarns.com
Haven

Somerset Designs
www.somersetdesigns.com
Suede purse bottom, handles, and slipper soles

Spud and Chloë
www.spudandchloe.com
Sweater

Therm O Web
www.thermowebonline.com
Heat n Bond Lite

Universal Yarn
www.universalyarn.com
Blossom Street Collection Petals Socks, Classic Chunky, Cotton Supreme Batik, Soft Payette by Rozetti

Yarns of Italy
www.yarnsofitaly.com
Lunare, Romanza

Acknowledgments

Thanks to everyone at Martingale for seeing my vision in this book and allowing me to pursue it. Karen Soltys and Cathy Reitan, you've both been positive, encouraging, and supportive. Thank you.

Lots of thanks to my mom and the many friends who knit projects for this book: Vera Frase (Mom), Michele Carotti, Tammy Briner, Cheryl Taylor, Casey Zaring, Lori Kerby, Anya Konzi-Ashburn, and Christine Chen.

Special appreciation to contributing designer Janet Rehfeldt. Janet has been knitting and crocheting since the age of seven. She's the owner of Knitted Threads Designs, LLC, and is an author, designer, and instructor. Her designs and articles can be found in leading knitting and crochet publications. Crochet Pink, a companion book to this one, is her sixth book with Martingale.